Fowre

1. SYNTHESIZERS

PUBLICATION STUDIO HUDSON

Edited by Andrew Siskind
Cover artwork by Robbie Simon
Synth Illustrations by Christin Ripley
Album Illustrations by Matt Bua
Title page lettering by Walker Mettling
Proofreading by Katy Smith

PILOT EDITIONS
© 2016

ISBN: 978-1-62462-139-0

Designed, printed, and bound by Patrick Kiley
Publication Studio Hudson
137 2nd St.
Troy N.Y.

www.publicationstudio.biz
pshudson@publicationstudio.biz

Fowre is a series of four books about music of varying formats and sizes. The odd spelling of our title is the fourth Hindu-Arabic numeral itself, a spelling of Tudor vintage subjected to orthographic fermentation in the dusty basement of printed history. It comes from a now rare tract by the Elizabethan poet Edmund Spencer, *Fowre Hymns* (1596), whose digital presence has eclipsed its physical one. The uncanny mutability of words—even of a single word over time, forming a great multitude of varietals—inspires this sequence of publications drunk on the sound of strings, circuits and voices.

CONTENTS

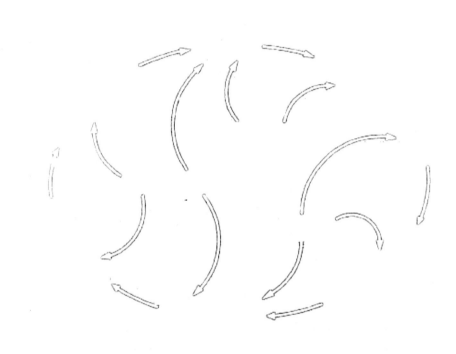

EDITOR'S NOTE

A sound synthesizer is an electronic musical instrument which generates, through one or more of several possible means, an electrical signal that when rendered audible by a speaker is perceived as musical (or decidedly non-musical) sound. Synthesizers have their roots in the 18th century, in the workshops of European madmen who charged the strings of their creations with electricity to create what they perceived as new qualities of sound. The earliest of these, Václav Prokop Diviš' "Denis d'or," or the "Golden Dionysus," literally shocked the player with every touch.

The history of the synthesizer is the work of another book. This collection of diverse material is like a small exhibition at a county art museum—drawn together and organized by topic, ringed around with a little prefatory or commentary material, but largely made available for you to dwell in and ruminate on at your leisure on the weekend, or if you get out of work early one day. Synthesizers fascinate us, I think, because they seem so otherworldly. They exist at the fringes of music, apart from wooden and brass instruments. They appeal to our fetishization of technology, of the other, and tempt us into the marginal space between what we can comfortably say is music and what we have our doubts about.

There is something essentialized, to me, about the way that synthesizers create music. They go straight to the source, pulling at the fabric of the world, allowing us to edit sound in an unimaginably rich way. But for all their perceived refinement over the trombone, they do fulfill the same role. In some ways they alienate the physicality of our bodies from the production of sound, something that an instrument we have to touch with our lips never would.

In a society where the things we physically interact with most are small computers without any moving parts, they are though perhaps a better symbolic object for the relationship between our bodies and the production of music than a trombone.

What, after all, could be said about these machines that interfere directly with electromagnetic fields, pulling and dragging energy which, pooling and overflowing, pours from the outlet on the wall through the device's narrow canyons and wide rippling ponds and out to sea; into a magnetic speaker that can translate the riparian fluctuations of electricity into patterns of audible sound? To document their cultural significance is the work of a braver man than I. They are still semi-magical to me. Confusing and mystifying, they obscure the source of musical sound behind a veil of technology and mysterious ritual which perhaps we hesitate to look beyond.

Inasmuch as there is a thesis underlying this project, it is that synthesizers are interesting to read about, and those people who create them, perform with them, or live with them in their home as "sonic furniture" are even more interesting to read about. This slim volume is hopefully many things to many people; first and foremost it is a talismanic object which offers certain abilities and protections to those who possess it, and secondly a collection of texts I hope will offer some insight into one of contemporary music's more obscure zones.

To briefly elaborate on the project's aims, I'll share some of the questions I hoped to find answers to in compiling this book, and hope that an outline traced around their scope might give you some rough shape of its material. Firstly, I wanted to know if synthesizers are in some essential way different from other musical instruments. What does the daily practice of a synthesizer-focused musician look like? Is it essentially different in any way from that of a cellist?

Secondly, I pushed all of the conversations captured in this book towards the place where the "natural world" and synthesizers meet. I did this because it seems like an interesting seam to examine. Synthesizers, to me, are systems; systems of systems, even. In that way I see them as modeling the natural world—Ammonsonian networks of causality and interactivity where small changes ripple outwards. And yet, synthesizers are distinctly "technological" in appearance, and I believe we put them in the mental category of inherently unnatural things, and I was curious to tug at this thread and see what developed.

I selected the contributors for this project using a highly refined and completely subjective process. Each one had said or written something in the past that piqued my interest, and I wanted only what all readers want—to speak with the author. In trying to ensure a diversity of voices I contacted both instrument creators and performers, and it's a testament to this field that almost everyone I reached out to was happy to participate. I'd like to thank all those involved for their time and for sharing their thoughts and ideas.

It's my hope that in these few pages you can find something interesting enough to tell a friend about later on in the day, when you meet them for coffee. This book is more about the synthesizer as is, or as Olivier Gillet says, "as a natural artifact," with which one develops a unique relationship as both a performer and a listener. I am a performer, an owner, an amateur enthusiast, and yet I wouldn't write a book about them as such—the natural limits of my scope, my skill, and my experience would circumscribe too narrow a field. What I've done here instead is to gather some diverse voices in the field, in conversation with me, with each other, and with their instruments. This is just one possible vision of the situation—not comprehensive, but hopefully representational.

– Andrew Siskind

"There is nothing to do and everything will get done."

– Suzanne Ciani

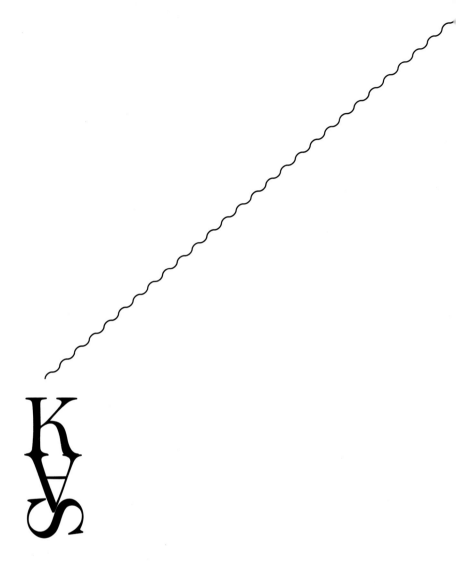

The first thing you might notice about Kaitlyn Aurelia Smith is her radiant blue/green aura. Beyond that, I won't reveal anything. Her work is intricate, but without seams, and intrinsically filled with joy. The spaces she creates through composition and performance are for us: to inhabit in wonder, to be challenged by, and renewed in. I am grateful to have had the opportunity to sit with her at a coffee shop in LA for an hour, and I present our conversation to you here.

kaitlyn aurelia smith

What was your first synthesizer?

I was so fortunate, and I'm very grateful, my first synthesizer was a Buchla 100. I didn't own it, it was a loaner from a neighbor, and I didn't even know what a Buchla was when he showed it to me.

Was there a steep learning curve?

When my friend lent me the Buchla, he didn't tell me anything about it. He just said, "here, borrow this for a year, explore." I was living by myself in a cabin so it was purely experiential and experimental. I had no idea what a lot of the Buchla synthesizer terminology meant. For a while, I made a bunch of sounds intuitively without paying too much attention to patching details. A few months into it, I realized that if I wanted to be able to recreate a sound I liked I'd need to know what's going on. So I'd go back and deduce what I was doing, and that's how I learned synthesis, by making a sound and then going back and figuring out what I had done.

Could you describe in some detail your current synth process or practice? The things you do every day, every week, associated rituals with electronic instruments, any aspects of your praxis and relationship to the machines?

PATCHING is the process of creating a signal path through a synthesizer, primarily using cables to connect various components.

"When I think about synthesis, I'm constantly thinking about how it relates to the voice, because every instrument is just an extension of the voice."

At the moment, I practice my live set every day because I have an album coming out in April and will be touring a lot this year. The live set is choreographed to line up with visuals so I'm practicing that everyday to keep it in my muscle memory.

Beyond that, mostly, it seems to be early morning or evening, two to four hours a day. I'll spend time just exploring a synth, a sound, an idea, a melody.

I'll also have freewriting sessions everyday, just compositionally thinking about what harmonic material I want to work with—this is usually with a piano/keyboard or notepad. Composition is my main focus in synthesis. I understand the technical stuff when I need to, but it's not the driving thing for me. That schedule is pretty regular for me, and then I have jobs that come through for composition so then I'll spend some time during the day working on those.

I'm interested in the idea of choreography when it comes to sets, can you expand on that at all? Are you physically doing the same actions each time or moving your body in a certain way in relationship to the instrument?

For this album I am. For the past six months it's been a daily routine to get it in my muscle memory. Also, the easel, right now the tuning has been really great, it's burned in really well, but the past few months I had to make sure I had three or four places in my set I had time to tune it on the fly if I needed to, so getting that into my muscle memory as well, knowing where my whole setup is if I need to tune, so then I can trust that my body will handle the motions without me needing to think about it.

It's always interesting for me to watch synthesizer performances that often don't involve a keyboard, but often do also, and to see what performers choose to do with their bodies. Do you have awareness of that, thinking about what to do with your body while you play the set?

I've never thought about, "What am I going to do while I'm playing the set to make it look interesting?" or any-

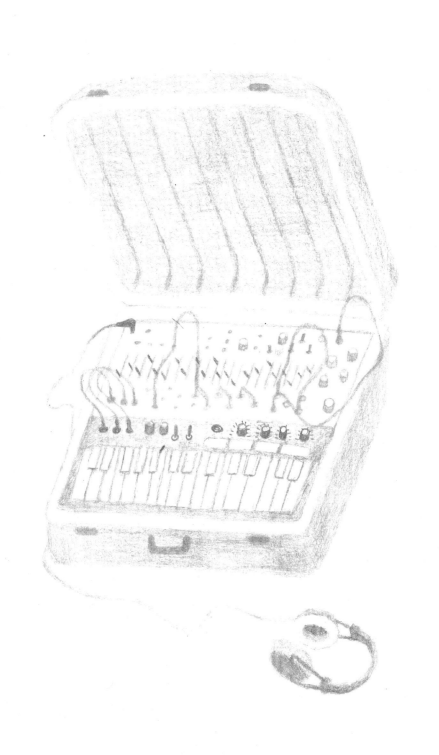

thing like that, and I used to do more patching during my live sets, but for this album it's one universal patch, and I'm more playing the easel like an instrument—knowing from memory how to quickly get the sound I want, doing alternate tunings…

What instrumental background do you come to synthesizers from, and do you think that background has shaped the way you interact with electronic instruments?

Definitely, yeah. I studied classical guitar at school, and then also played piano growing up, and I studied singing a little bit at Berklee, not very much. But I feel like, when I think about synthesis, I'm constantly thinking about how it relates to the voice, because every instrument is just an extension of the voice, or the human that can't make that sound, so I'm always trying to figure out what would be the connection from the human to the sound. I know it sounds abstract, but it's what I think about all the time—how to keep the human element connected.

How do you conceive of the relationship between the synthesizer as this contemporary electronic musical instrument, and the natural world, systems in nature, sounds in nature, things that are created organically?

HARMONICS are the integer multiples of the fundamental frequency, i.e. mathematically related frequencies. Some harmonics are pleasing to the human ear, and others are not.

Well, I want to think about that for a moment, because there's a few different answers that come to mind. The first thing that comes to mind, because I'm really fascinated by sound design and creation, I will do research sessions where I'll sit in nature and try and hear how many sounds are going on at once, how many layers, and try and identify a single source of the sound or if it's the harmonics crossing over each other that create that sound. So that's been definitely an influence for me when I approach synthesis, thinking about how certain natural sounds cross over one another to create their own sound. Conversely, when I'm analyzing a natural sound I'll think about it in synthesis terms. Does that make sense? I can't really do them easily in L.A., it was easier where I used to live because I was in a rural setting. I recently went to the Verdugo mountains, but the highway was right there. I mean those sounds are interesting to me too, but you asked about the natural world.

Another thing I like to do for research and sound design is change my listening environment. For example, I'll do an experiment to find out what certain things sound like when I'm underwater versus above water, and what they sound like during that transition, and think about how I can relate that to synthesis or composition, how can I recreate that sound? Or, changing head rotation and changing it fast or slow, ask myself: how can I resimulate all these things in synthesis and give people that experience that I just had? Resimulating those experiences are intriguing to me because I'm very interested in soundscapes, and into creating environments that feel transportive. On this new record, I really tried to do that.

Do you conceive of it as headphone music?

Not necessarily. It's funny, I used to, but now I'm having more fun figuring out techniques for giving people that spatial-audio sensation without it being in headphones. That's more of a challenge for myself. How can someone feel that it's above their head and behind their back, even if it's mono? That's been really weird and fun to play with.

I think of synthesizers as primarily instruments of organization, of systematics. Does that make any sense?

That's really interesting, I have to really think about that for a minute. The analogy I'm going to use here isn't necessarily a synthesis analogy, it's more of an audio engineering analogy, but it feels right, it speaks to me in terms of answering that question in all areas of my life including synthesis. I remember in one of my audio engineering classes they said, "every time that you boost or pull a frequency another one will pop up somewhere else." That's something that I think about a lot, in regards to synthesis and everything else in my life. If I change one thing, how is

"I'll do an experiment to find out what certain things sound like when I'm underwater versus above water, and what they sound like during that transition."

MONO means a monophonic recording in which all sounds are mixed together. By comparison, in a stereo recording some sounds are sent to the right speaker, and others to the left speaker.

"I really like when I listen to music and my brain can't figure it out, and I have to just surrender and listen."

A DUAL ARBITRARY FUNCTION GENERATOR (AWG) is a very complicated name for what is essentially a wonderfully unique sequencer.

it going to affect everything else, in passive ways and active ways? I try to find those effects and follow those pathways.

Is it always an unexpected result? Is there always an element of chance in any system?

It feels like a mixture of that, which is fun, like happy accidents, and chess. You're always trying to think ten steps ahead, and have the visual brain to know, "if I patch this to this, to this, to this," I'll get this effect. Or maybe not. The other side of that is not having it so well thought out, and just playing. It depends on what the results are that I want.

What's one synthesis term or word that you were stumped by?

In the Eurorack world, there's a lot of new creative terminology for something that already had a name that confuses me sometimes. I haven't really delved into that world besides playing Make Noise and studio electronics stuff. Serge modules that can do like twelve different things — those confused me.

In my mind whenever I play a new synthesizer I always relate it back to the way Buchla is set up, because that's my experience, so I'm always translating everything into that language. My favorite Buchla term is probably the "Dual Arbitrary Function Generator," it's amazing, it makes you sound like you're in a '70s sci fi. I want to answer your question though.

There was something that happened yesterday that was super helpful thanks to Tony at Make Noise. I was explaining to him a sound I used to really like on an Electrocomp I used to play — Tony read up on it and helped me to figure out how to recreate it on his Make Noise system. That is something that I look for, being able to be in contact with the maker. That's really special.

How do you maintain engagement with synthesizers over time?

I think because composition is my main focus, when I feel a little bit of a block there, I think of a new sound I can make—or change my focus. There's always deeper to go, and then of course when you get a new piece of equipment the novelty of figuring it out keeps me engaged.

What are some influences that you think people might not guess, hearing your recordings?

There's probably so many—I like such a variety of music. Michael Jackson, Beach Boys…D'Angelo. I'm obsessed with D'Angelo, Flying Lotus, Kendrick Lamar, I like those guys a lot.

I am very influenced by classical music—Ravel, John Adams, Hildegard Von Bingen, Jazz…In terms of visual artists, Moebius is a huge influence for me, Miyazaki as well. Kandinsky, philosophy books—anything that engages the inquisitive mind.

What is your favorite Miyazaki movie?

Nausicaa, which is actually what the new album is inspired by. I wanted to create an album that made one feel like they were on a motion ride in a futuristic jungle.

You said there were some visual elements to your new performance, can you elaborate on those at all?

At the moment, the visuals that I'm using for the live set are a collaboration with Sean Hellfritsch and Jeff Manson. I played them the album, exactly as I'll play it live, and then they created the visuals to be the exact timing.

What elements of synthesis are you currently most interested in?

I'm really interested in kind of confusing listeners in terms of what is synthesis and what is real, and creating sounds that sound like they're from nature. I never use outside samples, I always make my own sounds, I sample my

HILDEGARD VON BINGEN, also known as "Saint Hildegard" and "Sibyl of the Rhine," was a German Benedictine abbess, writer, composer, philosopher, Christian mystic, visionary, and polymath of the 12th century.

A SAMPLE is the result of the reduction of a continuous signal to a discrete signal; an individual audio or control voltage recording.

> "There's a scent I always try to conjure for my creativity, and it ignites it, and it's the smell of old books when you go through the pages really fast."

own stuff—I think it's important to make that distinction. I do my own field recordings of nature sounds.

I'm really interested in combining real instruments with synthesis. My new album has orchestral instruments on it, and I really enjoyed processing them in such a way so that you can't tell if it's a synthesizer or a bass clarinet, and layering them in such a way so that you can't really tell what each layer is. That's related to the thing I was talking about in sound design, sitting out in nature and hearing all the blends, and thinking, "what are the big sounds, and what are all the babies that they make together? Don't put that in, or do. Ha!"

Because of studying music and composition, when I'm listening to something I don't always have a clean slate, my brain is often trying to figure out, "what's going on there?" I really like when I listen to music and my brain can't figure it out, and I have to just surrender and listen—so that's become a goal, to make music that people can just listen to and not try and analyze. But if they want to try and analyze it, they can. But I also think it's so helpful, and it's how I learned, listening to other people and analyzing their music. That's how all artists learn from each other, finding something you like, analyzing it.

I stole this question from The Paris Review. *Is there a piece of equipment you always use first, and where do you work?*

I always use my voice first, or my head, my inner ear. Something that really helps me with writing is changing where I'm working, especially that feeling of setting up a new zone and everything is perfectly in it's place. But I always need to be able to see outside, that's something that's really important for me..

Do you recommend a specific type of incense?

I prefer candles—I really like vetiver and amber. I love palo santo. There's a scent I always try to conjure for my creativity, and it ignites it, and it's the smell of old books when you go through the pages really fast. There's such a nostalgic thing going on there for me.

Do you intuit or experience anything special or idiosyncratic about the relationship between your body and the synthesizer?

I get this really specific feeling in my hand when I see a module or anything that has lots of tactile things. The more it has to interact with, the more my hands get this weird sensation—a tingle/itch. It's not limited to synthesizers, I also get it with books—old kids books with envelopes you have to open, things that are very interactive, my hands get really excited.

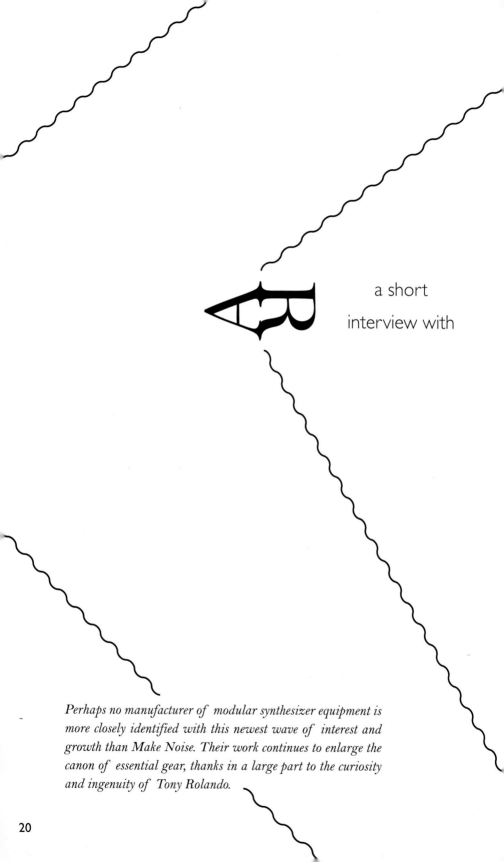

a short

interview with

Perhaps no manufacturer of modular synthesizer equipment is more closely identified with this newest wave of interest and growth than Make Noise. Their work continues to enlarge the canon of essential gear, thanks in a large part to the curiosity and ingenuity of Tony Rolando.

anthony rolando

How has your personal practice as a musician and performer shaped your hand as a designer of synthesizer technology?

I get overwhelmed by large, complicated studio environments. I've always preferred focused situations for musical experience. I think this is why I always liked the "suitcase synth" (a.k.a the portable 6U or 7U Eurorack system). I'm inspired by the challenge of working within some set of limitations to create something that far exceeds what people believed possible. I believe this is where some magic and inspiration is discovered.

Does your experience with electronic musical instruments impact in any way your understanding of the natural world?

I feel synthesizers allow us to recreate and amplify perceived natural phenomenon. Each of us feels and hears the natural world differently and a synthesizer could be an instrument for sharing how we understand the natural world. It allows us to re-create the sounds and feelings but in a more dramatic way which could reflect our own emotional movements as we experience the natural world.

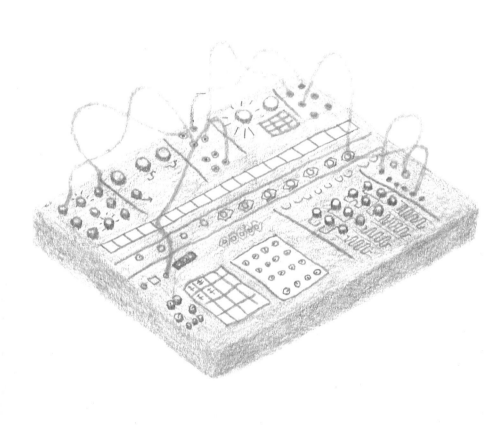

If there's one core element you think is essential to the design of a useful, successful electronic instrument or module, what would you say that is?

A successful module and successful instrument might be two different things…generally I believe you must consider all of the obvious uses and then attempt to plan for uses which you do not yet understand by installing wildcards wherever possible. Perhaps these wildcards seem useless at the moment, but at some point they could define a new musical movement, or at least a new musical motif.

How do you feel the role of a synthesizer developer has changed, if at all, in the last fifty years?

I do not think the role of the designer has changed much at all. Music has changed far more. As designers we are still just trying to capture the hearts of musicians with potential for inspiration.

"Each of us feels and hears the natural world differently and a synthesizer could be an instrument for sharing how we understand the natural world."

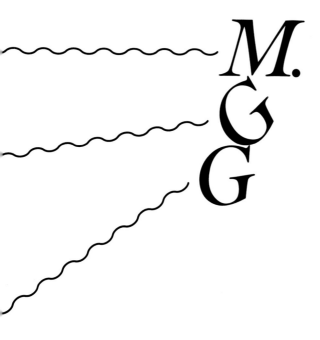

M. Geddes Gengras cuts a lean shadow across the East L.A. landscape, iced coffee in one hand, cigarette in the other, smiling wryly under big sunglasses. He's one of the few people I know who wears Grateful Dead shirts more frequently than I do. Around his neck there are several small medallions.

Once, years ago, I saw him perform live for the first time at the Upstate Artists Guild in Albany, NY. The presenter introduced him as an "International Synth Wizard," and everybody nodded in agreement. His music is frighteningly immersive, hypnotic, moving smoothly along the subtle continuum between the terrifyingly uncanny and the blissfully serene.

ONE

There's this problem—when an audience looks at people using gear like that, using modular synthesizers, they kind of assume they're not doing anything, that the machine is making the music. Which is partially true, for sure, the machine has a big part in the music, or at least is playing the music to a degree, but it's the same association people have with laptop musicians too. You know, you just click around.

For me, when Ishi came out a couple years ago, there was a lot of discussion in my apartment between my roommate Nick Wallas and I about how you had made it. Specifically we were trying to decode what was synthesizers, what was computers, etc.

Well, there's at least one piece of mystery rack gear on that. But really, the process was so simple for that record that I might've been a little more guarded about how it was done, because it was really, really stripped down compared to what I usually do with synths. 95% of that record is just a monosynth, either a Moog or the Arturia, and then a really simple patch with three modules: a Make Noise Phonogene doing the sampling of what I was playing in real time, using a Make Noise Wogglebug to sort of randomly select when it would sample, and to manipulate the sample length and grain size and all that stuff, and then just letting that run. Then it was just a matter of sitting down and playing, doing a bunch of different takes of improvising melodies into that chain, and a couple of them just came out and sounded crazy. And the other ones just didn't really work, you know?

A MONOSYNTH is a one-voice synthesizer, based around a single oscillator or other sound source. Notably, a monosynth can only play a one note at a time.

A MODULE is an individual synthesizer hardware component. Modular synthesizer systems combine circuits designed and built by one or many different individuals to create a complete, unique instrument.

We definitely got into a deep debate about whether or not you had made the record with computer software like Ableton.

No, no Ableton. I've never made a record with Ableton. I've used it on records before, I used it on the Congos record a little bit, but that was the free version. I couldn't even export tracks, I was plugging my headphone jack into my tape deck, you know? I would love to learn it, and I feel like once I do learn it I'll feel like, "What the fuck have I been doing for the past ten years?"

Is there any software you do deploy regularly?

I've been using Pro Tools for a long time. When it comes to computer software, at this point, they're all basically the same. It's just a matter of what features are in there, and what you're comfortable using. Recently I got a new computer, and it didn't have Pro Tools on it, and I've been using Pro Tools for a decade and I thought, "I'm not going to get Pro Tools this time, fuck Pro Tools, I'm done with it." And I tried everything else, and they're all basically the same. But in the end I'm so comfortable with it, I know the shortcuts, and I don't want to spend even another five months trying to learn another one, it seems like a monumental waste of time. I have no problems with the way Pro Tools works.

Do you always record your own work, or have you spent time in other people's studios?

I've done it before, with bands, going into a studio to do that. And it's so nice, but for me recording is such a big part of making music, and recording it myself. Especially back when there was no possibility of anybody putting it out or any way to make any money back off of it, going into a studio just seemed like a really unnecessary expense. Also, the way I make music, I don't think I could work on a schedule like that, or with those sort of constraints. It seems really stressful to me. I'd love to do it again, and go in and do stuff specifically in a studio space and use it for what it is, but I

"I feel like once I do learn it I'll feel like, 'What the fuck have I been doing for the past ten years?'"

learned pretty quickly that for what I'm doing I don't need much gear. I need a couple of pieces of gear, a couple nice preamps and a nice compressor and that's really it. I rarely am ever doing more than two tracks at a time.

What was your first synthesizer?

It was a Moog Rogue. I bought it on eBay around 1999, back in the wild days of eBay when things were cheap. Maybe I paid $400 for it? Which was a ton of money for me. It was my first musical instrument.

You didn't play guitar or something before that?

No, my brother did. He started playing guitar around that same time. I guess I'd say I was a pretty late bloomer when it comes to music, I wasn't into music when I was a kid. Even during early adolescence, it didn't really interest me much.

Was there something else, artistically, you were primarily engaged with?

I was really into comic books, I was really into Sci-Fi, Star Wars, shit like that. I was really into the X-Files. I was a nerd, you know? I was a nerdy kid. As far as music goes, I liked some of the stuff my dad listened to, but I had a lot of friends who were into current stuff. I think I was in fifth grade when Kurt Cobain died, and I had a bunch of friends who were big Nirvana fans already, and I just didn't understand at all. I was like, "What do you guys like about this?" I didn't like it because my dad hated it, so I always thought it was garbage. Once I turned 17 though, it changed to "Nirvana's the best!"

So why did you buy the Moog?

So, I started getting into music right around the time I started High School. I had a friend who was a big music nerd, and his entry into it was Nirvana and then he went to the next level thing, which was to read about all the bands Kurt was listening to, and then to try and find all this stuff, which at the time was difficult. I remember it took us a year to find a Young Marble Giants CD, or finding Can records. We got Ege Bamyasi, but we'd been looking for it for like eight months.

That's a feeling that's almost completely gone from our society.

That's something that's hard to experience lately, just sitting down with those things, putting the CD in and thinking, "Oh my god, oh my god!" I don't remember the last time I had that feeling, maybe when Dave's Picks shows up. So this guy was making me all these tapes, and turning me on to a lot of really amazing stuff, sort of the contemporary '90s indie stuff. Pavement, Yo La Tengo, and Stereolab. Stereolab and Silver Apples were the two things that he turned me on to that really flipped my lid pretty hard, and especially in Stereolab I was just blown away. I knew they were using synthesizers, and I went and saw them play, and I couldn't figure out what the synths were doing.

The entire massive sound they were making I liked so much, and they have a song with "Moog" in the name, and I saw them play and they had the Moog and I wasn't sure what it was doing but I thought, "If I get one of these things, I'll probably sound sort of like this band," you know? What I thought was the Moog then though was really the Farfisa or something like that, but I bought the Moog.

I saved up money, and I borrowed a little money from my dad, and bought the thing. I had it for two or three weeks before I figured out how to get it to stop making sound. There's a switch you had to turn off to make it not just be playing, droning, all the time. And that was weeks of my life. I'd turn it on and right away it'd be making this noise, and I'd panic a little and turn it off again. But I wasn't—you know, I had no musical training, I had no lessons in anything. No keyboard, piano lessons, whatever.

So you approached this instrument with only your image of

"I had no musical training, I had no lessons in anything. No keyboard, piano lessons, whatever... But a Moog makes that okay..."

> "I developed this style that might not be unique to me but is unique to these instruments, a sort of legato, constantly moving melody."

it and intuited how it worked?

But a Moog makes that okay, because all of a sudden you're dealing with a different set of parameters, it's not just notes you can play. Actually those first couple weeks when it would just drone a note all the time, I spent so much time playing with the other controls, trying to figure out what they did. I messed around with it a bunch, I used it in some very casual high school bands and recording projects and things, and then I kind of put it away. I got really into hardcore, I started playing in hardcore bands and it just got stuck in a closet in my house for a while and I didn't really fuck with it for a long time.

Probably around 2003 - 2004, I started to get interested in other kinds of music again. I came out of that black hole of extremity, but I think it was a great thing for me. I feel like all of my values around music, artistic expression, and the way you conduct yourself as a musician or a band comes from that world. I find that most of the people I gravitate to in the music scene were involved in that world too, in one way or another. In a lot of ways it reminds me of the way I feel about Deadheads too, it's a similar thing, a very strong, fierce D.I.Y., independent ethos, you know? People creating a subculture and inhabiting it, making it their home.

Do you think your approach to synthesis is distinct in some way from other artists because it was your first instrument? There aren't a lot of other people out there, at least that I've met or heard of, who went straight from nothing to synthesizers.

Yeah, I do. I talk about this with the Moog guys a lot. I think a lot of the people they work with, most musicians who play synthesizers, are coming to it from something else. Guitar players, mostly keyboard players. I think it's exciting to see people who really are synthesists, that is their instrument, that's their palette. When you take the technical proficiency of keyboardists out of that, you're left with this very open range of what performance can be, what those sounds can be, and what you can do with them. Not that I'm against keyboards—I use keyboards all the time.

Have you become a proficient keyboardist?

I've become proficient in a very limited sense. I can't... I can play with myself, that's about it. I feel like learning to play keyboard the way I did on the Moog was a really broken way to do it, and probably in a lot of ways stunted my understanding of theory or whatever, which I still don't really have any real understanding of. Everything, all that stuff, whenever it's deployed in my music it's on an intuitive basis. I'm not trying to brag, I just really don't know that stuff at all. You could sit me down and ask me what scale or key I'm playing in and I honestly don't know. So I'm proficient to a degree, but when you put me with other musicians and ask me to play a song, that could be rough.

I play by myself, and people see me play and think I must've taken lessons, and the truth is I just learned how to do this one very specific thing, based around the architecture of these synthesizers, based around being able to play one note at a time. So, learning to play one-handed a lot, because the other hand is on parameter patrol, I developed this style that might not be unique to me but is unique to these instruments, a sort of legato, constantly moving melody. I was gripping hard from people like Terry Riley. But no, I don't really consider myself a keyboard player–I use keyboards, and I like them, I like the tactile response of it and I like being able to improvise on them, but I don't really know how to play them.

Is Terry Riley a major influence? If I had to guess, I'd say you had a nice stack of Terry's records at home. Have you ever seen him perform live? I was completely floored when I realized he was playing those long strings of notes live, with his hands, and not just using a sequencer or even an arpeggiator.

Oh yeah. It's unreal to watch him play. He can also transpose into any key at any point, he's a genius. There was one aspect to his music that really sticks with me, the

"...the endless stream of notes and the feeling of the way the patterns are constructed, the overall heave of the thing..."

In the context of synthesizers, a PARAMETER is any individual thing that can be adjusted to alter the sound. In a monosynth environment like the Moog Rogue, each parameter is generally represented by a single knob, switch, or button.

> "I had been singing in bands for years, and I thought, 'I want to play guitar, I want to play an instrument.' I was tired of not having that sort of input into the music."

endless stream of notes and the feeling of the way the patterns are constructed, the overall heave of the thing, that I really gravitated towards and tried to master. He's one of those guys—listening to that stuff, it boggles my mind how anyone could even think that quickly. It brings me back to Jerry too. It's premental play, playing before forethought. The body becomes so attuned to the action that you can operate on a premental level.

So, do you still own that Moog Rogue?

Yeah, I never got rid of it. I've thought about selling it several times, but every time it comes down to it I just have a really hard time. It's, you know, it's pretty nostalgic for me. It's my first musical instrument. I feel like a lot of people don't actually keep those, though.

I broke my first acoustic guitar, and I sold my first electric guitar last year. It was kind of a bittersweet process. I've thought a lot about selling my first synthesizer, but I can't seem to justify it when I still don't totally understand everything it might be capable of. How did you progress from the Moog Rogue to patchable, modular synthesizers?

Well, post Hardcore band life I started making music on my own again, living in upstate New York. I got my first looping pedal, which was a really big step, and I had a guitar. I'd started playing guitar, I was playing in a band around that time—I just started learning. I was playing in this really sort of simple, kind of stoner metal band that was great. Basically everybody in the band was really great at playing music except for me, but it was cool because the songs were simple enough that I could hang, and everybody wanted me to be in the band anyways. I had been singing in bands for years, and I thought, "I want to play guitar, I want to play an instrument." I was tired of not having that sort of input into the music.

And then around that time I was starting to get the synthesizer out again, I was playing with the guitar and loop pedals, and tapes, and the four track recorder—the four track was another thing, I got that around the same time I got the Moog basically, the Moog and the four track and my first delay pedal. I look back on that now, and obviously that is the genesis of this whole damn thing. So yeah, getting that stuff out again, especially the four track that I hadn't touched in years, because all of a sudden I was playing in this crazy loud six-piece hardcore band. I thought, "you can't record that with a four track, this thing is useless," and it sat in a closet for a long time until I started making music by myself again.

I think maybe that's a phenomenon that deserves a name: coming back into contact with gear that's been left behind, and suddenly what wasn't really clicking before becomes totally fundamental. So what got it back out into the world, or you back into its world?

I just got—I don't know—I was in this zone where the band I was in wasn't that active, I had a lot of free time, I was working. I just had a lot of time on my own. I was getting back into music again, listening to new things, starting to really get into psychedelia for the first time, diving into '60s and '70s stuff. I don't know why, or how it happened, but at a certain point I was making a lot of music by myself, and I got really into that process. It was all pretty terrible, but I was pretty into doing it, working on it, and sort of obsessively tweaking these little things. Playing with sounds. A lot of stuff that I do now came from that time of learning how to play with the four track, and how to play with recording as an instrument.

And then I moved out to LA, and then pretty quickly things picked up. Obviously there's a ton of stuff going on out here, and in 2005 when I moved out here there was a lot of really cool shit going on. Echo Curio opened right when I moved out here, and that was for a long time one of the hubs for interesting, underground stuff in LA. I got exposed to the local scene—Not Not Fun, Il Corral, The Smell—stuff like that. At that point I was doing music by myself, and I was playing music with my brother Cyrus—we were doing stuff mostly in the psychedelic folk music

"I was just blown away by the fact that you could do it 'wrong' but that still did something."

A MODULAR synthesizer system is an instrument built out of individual, discrete modules. The control and audio signals can be routed freely throughout the system to achieve a variety of different configurations.

A SERGE SYNTHESIZ-ER is a modular system designed by, or based on designs by, former Cal Arts professor Serge Tcherepnin. Powerful, id-iosyncratic, and uniquely affordable compared to classic Moog and Buchla modular systems, origi-nal Serge equipment is now highly sought after.

/ freak folk / free folk idiom. We were really into Six Or-gans [of Admittance], Matt Valentine, Double Leopards, No Neck Blues Band—stuff like that. Definitely a strong northeast vibe.

So the moment was ripe for you to get into something new?

Around that time a really good friend of mine who lives in Hudson, a buddy of mine from when I was living around there, came to visit and he had just started building his first modular system. It was a little Doepfer case, and I had seen modular synthesizers before but I had never played with one. They had a Serge system at Bard that I spent maybe a few hours once trying to figure out how it worked and could get nowhere with it, like absolutely never got a sound to come out of the damn thing.

This is the first time I really ever sat down and played with one. My friend was showing me all the shit you could do, and plugging things in the wrong way—you know, you can plug the audio into the input of the filter, or you could plug the audio into the CV of the filter and it does this—and I was just blown away by the fact that you could do it "wrong" but that still did something. Around this time I had started to feel the limitations of the Moogs. I had been making a lot of music with them, I had released a lot of tapes around that time of very simple set-up stuff, Moog and a long chain of delays, loopers, reverbs, etc. to create these—well I called it "cloud music," it was like power am-bient or something. It was pretty, and it had that sort of vaguely orchestral vibe to it, but it was also sort of lo-fi and driven, and blasted a little bit.

The kind of shit that now you can make with one Eurorack module.

Right. I was just starting to feel like I was hitting the wall with what I could do as a keyboard player, and I was getting a lot better in that time but part of getting better was realizing, "If I don't start to learn some theory, all my stuff is going to start sounding the same." The shows were getting better, but I was starting to get less interested in it. I wanted to keep working in that world, because I was very attached to the process of synthesis, and also all the work I had put into learning it. I love the fine touch, the very tactile aspect of getting really tuned in to your instrument.

So: you were getting tired of the limitations of the Moog + outboard effects zone?

Yeah, and even more than that I was hitting my own limitations. Compositional limitations, what I was able to accomplish through improvisation. What I was able to accomplish through a combination of improvisation and what I knew about music up to that point. And I was getting tired of the playing. I realized the thing I was interested in was the sound, and the thing that I was losing interest in was the playing part. Even what the notes were, that started to matter less and less to me, and even though I knew I had to keep a hand on the keyboard obviously because something has to be happening, it was getting less interesting to me. Right around that time I found modular synthesizers.

How did modular equipment enter your world?

When I started building my first system and using it for gigs, it was for a long time always an accessory to the main thing. There was always the same set up with the Moogs and the delays, and then the modular was just added color. I used it to make little sounds or to add ambiance to things. But once I started getting into it, I got deeper and deeper. In 2011/2012 I ended up having to go back to Connecticut unexpectedly for two months. My dad had a big health thing and was in the hospital, and then was recovering in a convalescent home for a while so I moved back home temporarily to take care of his place and help him out. You know, be there for him – I'd take him out to smoke cigarettes during the day, drive him out of the old folks' home so he could have a smoke, things like that.

While I was there staying at my dad's place I kind of went insane, as one might do in a situation like that when

In the context of modular synthesis, OUTBOARD EFFECTS are any signal processing devices not in modular form within the system. These include things like external reverb, compression, delay, etc.

"I realized the thing I was interested in was the sound, and the thing that I was losing interest in was the playing part."

"I made a record, a tape, called *Empty Space* in about two days. I think that record is, for me, the break-through."

you're in the town where you grew up for two months in the summer all by yourself. I wouldn't see another person that I knew except for my dad for weeks at a time sometimes. I got really, really hermit-like. I was staying in my dad's apartment, and the only piece of gear I had brought with me was my modular, because I couldn't really bring my whole set-up. I figured I'd bring it so at least I had something to play with. I didn't even bring anything to record with.

Sometimes the best environments to do serious work in are the ones you expect to be the most casual.

After a couple weeks there I'm losing my fucking mind. I went and bought a little portable Boss recorder so I could record, and I made a record, a tape, called *Empty Space* in about two days. I think that record is, for me, the break-through—it's the first thing that I made that was strictly modular, and I think it was the first release where I figured out composition on that device in a real way. Even though I had had it for a few years at this point, being forced to use it exclusively really flipped around my whole conception of how I made music, and what I was doing. It was a really complex combination of factors, but my mental state at the time—I was in this space where I was ready to hone in on anything, pay attention to anything else—and the modular was there at the right time. The place I was in mentally was a very—you know, it was kind of dark and desolate —lonely? I found this place in the instrument that really expressed that. It's one of the first things I made where, even now when I listen to it, I'm immediately right back where I was when I made it. Inasmuch as a very abstract electronic 93-minute cassette of modular sounds can be, it's probably the most autobiographical thing I had done up until that point, and probably was until *Ishi*. In some ways maybe even more so—there's stuff in there, recordings of the place I was staying, things embedded in that record.

That sounds like a transformative moment. So that was the moment when you embraced the techniques you deploy today?

It was a huge sea change for me. At that point I thought, 'okay, yeah, this is what I'm doing with music.' I put the Moogs away for a few years at that point, and really doubled down on the modular, spending all my time trying to learn the ins and outs of how it worked. I got obsessed with this idea of using the synthesizer for creating systems to compose music automatically. Going back to what I was talking about earlier, about getting bored of playing the keyboard, well now I didn't have to play the notes anymore. I don't even have to pick when the notes come—I just tell it what notes it's allowed to play, and let it run.

It was probably a few years before anything good emerged from that, but it was a fascinating learning process. I found that when I was playing with this thing, I'd spend hours and hours on the same simple patch, listening to it, listening to it, listening to it. I became so fascinated by the sounds it made. When I was staying in Connecticut, that was when I started just leaving my synthesizer on all the time, running, and it's been that way ever since. At any given time, unless it's packed up, it's probably on, in my studio, running—you just have to walk in and push up a fader and it's going.

That's going to blow our readers' minds I think. Maybe not, but it definitely blew mine a little. It's so different from what's possible with a guitar or a harp, which you can't just "leave running" and step outside of and listen to.

When I saw Suzanne [Ciani] talk, she did a presentation at Cinefamily a couple years ago on the Buchla synthesizer, explaining how she used it, and she talked about that same thing. She talked about how she'd leave it on for days and days, and it was like a piece of furniture in her house, it was like sonic furniture. Afterwards I went outside, I saw her and I grabbed her and told her I'd nearly lost my mind when she said that because I'd never heard anybody describe the way I feel about this machine in a clearer way.

"It was a huge sea change for me. At that point I thought, 'okay, yeah, this is what I'm doing with music.'"

A FADER is a mechanical device for adjusting the intensity of a parameter, e.g., volume.

TWO

"I need to be able to go in and be playing with some-thing and be able to turn around, touch five things, and it's going— otherwise I'd never record."

This is a boilerplate question. Can you describe your current daily synth practice?

It definitely varies a lot, but I work in patterns—it's big waves for me. I will work a lot and I'll play a lot for long pe-riods of time, and then I'll go weeks, sometimes a month or two, especially if I don't have shows or I'm not working on a record. I'll go a while without touching it. Which is good. I used to get really stressed out about [not working] and I don't any more, I realized I need a kind of recharge peri-od to get back to where I'm at. But when I'm working it's very much an in and out thing. I have a room in my house that's the designated studio space, and everything is setup to record all the time, which is great. I need that. I need to be able to go in and be playing with something and be able to turn around, touch five things, and it's going—otherwise I'd never record. And even then I don't do it half the time, because that's even too much. So I try to make it as simple for myself as possible, because...the shit that I haven't re-corded, man, I think about that shit all the time. It's lost, especially with the modular synths, because you can't go back, you never go back. And there are some sounds that just exist on one recording I made and I would give any-thing to be able to figure out how I did that again.

Do you have an archival process? Are you constantly making reference recordings for yourself?

Yes, I record. When I'm good, I'm recording basically every patch I make.

Do you write patch notes as well?

No, unless it's something I know I'm going to attempt to recreate. For example, for doing the Personable stuff for instance there's specific routing, I'm using MIDI to connect different devices, I know that the signal needs to go to this oscillator and then this envelope, etc. For that I have a little cheat sheet, but for other stuff—any time I'm playing a show in L.A., I'm writing a piece, a patch, for that show.

And I try to do that anytime I play a show. Obviously when you go on tour it's not always feasible to do that, but I still try to as much as possible. What usually ends up happening is that I write a new piece every three or four shows when I have the time to yank everything and put it all back together.

A lot of those pieces will have small patches within the system that I use over and over again. I've definitely built the system in a lot of ways towards these patches, so it's kind of designed to do them.

So what does your practice look like at home, when you're not on the road?

I tend to work, when I'm working, at night. Although, these days it's changed and it's morning more than anything now. For a long time though I would always work on stuff at night, when people in the house were asleep. That's my go-to vibe.

Headphones?

No, monitors. I never really blast it, and I'm lucky the way my house is set up I have a door I can close and it won't really bother anybody if I'm making noise. I work on a piece all day, but a lot of times I'm not even in the studio for more than ten or fifteen minutes at a time because I'm doing twenty other things. Especially these days, I'm so busy with other stuff related to music that the actual making of music kind of gets squeezed into the cracks between writing emails and making phone calls and trying to get work done.

You're a busy man these days between working on your own projects and things with other musicians.

MIDI (Musical Instrument Digital Interface) is a standard electronic system of communication between musical devices.

Generally, an OSCILLATOR is understood to be a circuit that generates an audible tone by creating a periodic, oscillating electric current.

ENVELOPE is a term used to describe the attack, decay, sustain, and release of a sound. With a keyboard instrument, attack is how quickly a sound reaches its loudest point after the key is pressed, decay is how long it takes for a sound to decrease in volume to the level it will be sustained at, sustain is the volume it will remain at until the key is released, and release is how long it takes for the sound to decrease in volume back to silence after the key is released.

> ## "I'm trying to make functional music, music *for* something, whether it's music for dancing or music for relaxation, or whatever— it should do something."

I have a label called Duppy Gun that releases dub music, and that's been so much work lately. We're doing so much right now, we're really trying to gear up for a big launch, so my own music gets worked on in the cracks. But that's what I love about my system, I can leave it on, leave it running, and when I'm walking around doing something else and I think, "you know what would be cool, if I went in and connected this thing to that thing and I make this change," and I'll go in and do it and then just let it keep running and sit with it for a while. Or I'll just walk back out of the room, go back to doing something else.

Once I feel like I'm onto something though, it changes a little. Making records comes out of that process for me. Recording stuff randomly, and then at a certain point I start trying to stick things together. Aside from Ishi, which was made all in one go, very purposefully, every other record I've made has come together the opposite way. Combing through months, or even years, of records, and sticking things together. Dropping tracks on top of other tracks just to see what it sounds like, even if they're recorded three years apart from each other.

If it sounds great, I'll keep going with it. And if only five seconds of that sounds great, I'll grab those five seconds and keep moving. It's more of a collage, a long term process, and one that's been slowing down recently. The record that I just finished is five years worth of recordings, and I've finally done ten different versions of it. I feel like it's finally, actually done. I just kept making small tweaks, adding new things, deleting huge chunks of it. I mean at one point it was a single LP and now it's a double LP with only six minutes of material from that earlier draft on it, spread out throughout.

For me, making records is the ultimate part of it, my favorite part of it. Recording is such a personal, solitary time for me. It's beautiful, quiet, reflective time. Working on music in general, more than anything, is a meditative practice. If nobody was interested in what I was doing, and I was just doing it for myself, I'd probably still do it in pretty much the same way because it's become such a big part of my routine, and how I process different things happening in my life, how I work through…anything? It's like therapy, it's how I process my experiences, my emotions.

So your synth practice is how you contextualize your entire experience of life?

Yeah. I think that's how most artistic practices are at their core, right? I think it gets trickier when it's an art that's more abstract, as compared to a singer-songwriter writing a song about something that happened to them. I'm asking you to engage in this material that's maybe a little less easily apprehended, but ideally, my intention is coming through.

It's always really interesting to me to talk to people who listen to my music, about their experience with it, and how they use it. What they use it for. Because to a degree I'm trying to make functional music, music for something, whether it's music for dancing or music for relaxation, or whatever—it should do something. I don't want it to be useless. It needs to do something to you. Ishi is a great example—a lot of people I've talked to have told me something like, "I listen to that record every time I have a panic attack, I put on that record and it's like taking a Xanax or something."

And that's great, because for me that's what it was. I was really overwhelmed with things going on in my life at that point, and I had to do something with it. I'm pretty bad at just sitting on that stuff, trying to internalize it. So sticking to my practice has a lot of benefits for me, aside from my career. It's more of a basic need than that, and if it wasn't music it would be something else. I really believe that.

Before I was doing music I was doing theater, and I was really involved in that, and I think the only reason I pivoted to music, aside from the fact that I thought it was "cooler," was that it was something that you could do on your own. Theater takes so much infrastructure. I went to college to study theater, and I realized it's such an insane bureaucracy. So much stuff has to get done to make a piece of theater happen. You need twelve other people, at least, and an audience. You need an audience to do theater, but you don't

"You need an audience to do the-ater, but you don't need one to make music."

need one to make music. It's the last thing you need. You can be your own audience, and I was for a long time. I was my entire audience.

THREE

"…it's this idea that I'm not writing a song, I'm building a room."

Could you expand a little bit on the way you conceive of the relationship between theater and music? I think that was an interesting node we touched on earlier.

The most immediate connection that comes to my mind is that theater was how I got hooked on performing in front of people, and it was a huge ego boost. I was an awkward, nerdy kid. I was the smallest kid in my class. I had friends, but I wasn't popular. I always felt very out of place, and theater was definitely the first time I was getting positive feedback from my peers, from adults. I wasn't very good at sports, I don't know if you can tell.

For whatever reason, for very specific reasons I think, I was maybe a little more emotionally mature than other kids my age because of shit in my life I'd had to deal with early on. I was maybe a little more prepared to take on the heavy emotional lifting of doing theater at an age when kids are interested in it but on more of a surface level. You don't meet a lot of kids in junior high or even high school who really can do serious stuff. I'm not saying I was good, but I was really committed to it, and I took it very seriously.

I did *The Crucible* when I was 15 years old, not even five feet tall probably yet. That's what I was into, heavy shit. Theater was the first time I ever found anything I wanted to work hard on. It was the first time I really wanted to be good at something. I wanted to be the best at it. I wanted to be the best actor in my school. I wanted to do it really well.

Were you the best actor in your school?

Totally. Straight up, I was. At least, the best male actor. There were some really great female actors. People who still work in theater. I went to kind of an artsy high school, a lot of people did theater. It was run by ex-Quakers, it had very similar vibes to a Friends Academy. It had originally been a weird boarding school for sick and insane kids, with a farm, and they turned it into a weird hippie-d out semi-boarding school. They had like ten boarding students. My graduating class was around 26 kids.

Tiny school with a really strong focus on arts. They actually had a program called the creative arts program where you could basically work to earn a second diploma for arts stuff—so I did that for theater. A full 20-30 hours of work a week on theater in addition to the regular curriculum. And I was someone who before that could not be asked to do homework, or anything, ever. Where I grew up in Connecticut, I went to a private school because my parents both worked there. And there's an expectation that after you go to private elementary school you go on to private high school, prep school, etc. I applied to a bunch of those schools, but none of them wanted to let me in. I'm sure they looked at me and thought, "this kid is fucking nuts, he's damaged."

So the school I went to, Watkinson, they wanted me there. They were stoked to have me.

That's so rare and awesome. I feel like in mainstream education, high school students don't often feel like their teachers are stoked to be working with them. That's not a potshot at teachers, it's more of a commentary on the way our current educational model is set up.

When I talk about high school with people, I think about how lucky I was. Everybody I talk to who didn't go to school with me seems to have had a terrible time. For me, high school was chill as hell. It was a lot of work, but I had teachers who were really interested in encouraging me to do interesting, hard work. They also told me to stay away from music and concentrate on theater though, because music was clearly not my strongest suit. Can't be right all the

"...when you're working with sound, you're working with waves. And when you're working with synthesizers you're working with very basic elemental forces—it's electricity, voltage."

"...I look at a guitar player and think, 'how do you remember where all those notes are on the fretboard?'"

time. It was the perfect combination of high expectations in some areas but also letting me slide on other things. It made me believe I needed to be an artist, and that I had to do this.

Looping back though to the link between theater and music, what I really learned to appreciate about good theater, learning about it back then, seeing films of Peter Brook productions, never missing a show at Yale Rep Theater and Hartford Stage, while also going to hardcore and indie shows, was that theater presentations are so powerful because they're using all of the elements. Nothing's off limits, you can use any sensation to grab an audience. Music is maybe a little more narrow, at least in its traditional presentation.

There was something that appealed to me about the way you could create a world with theater. You don't just create a scene, you create an entire planet by extension, even if it's only barely hinted at or not mentioned at all, it exists. It exists automatically. So getting into music, getting back into music, trying to figure out what my thing was—it's this idea that I'm not writing a song, I'm building a room. I'm building an environment. Cameron [Stallones] & I talk about this a lot, creating an "interior architecture."

It's a place you can go into, and you can leave it, you can sit in it, you can have whatever experience you want. And ideally it's the kind of place where depending on what direction you're looking you can have a different experience of it, so you can keep going back in time and time again and keep pulling something new out of it. It's really environmental to me, and that's why I've moved away from traditional song structures as I go. I envision it as a bunch of distinct spaces, with a distinct physicality. I need to be able to step inside them myself to think it's going to work.

Can you speak about the relationship between synthesis, synthesizers, and the natural world? The topic has been on my mind a lot lately.

For starters I think developing an interest and an ear for ambient sound was a huge thing for me. Being unafraid to be unmusical is a big part of that too, because when you're working with sound, you're working with waves. And when you're working with synthesizers you're working with very basic elemental forces—it's electricity, voltage.

There's a connection that exists, that feels biological to me, like an extension of human biology. I think any instrument becomes an extension of the physicality of the person who plays it, but a synthesizer goes a level deeper because it has that tactile interface and that same intuition between the player and the instrument, but with the added layer of programming and sound design that goes into it.

Natural sound, or nature sounds, are a big influence on me. The way you listen to nature sounds, ambient sounds, is something I'm always trying to emulate in music. I like being unclear about what sounds are, where they're coming from, and how they're made. I think there's also something about the way the mind grows to accommodate that process as a musician and the way that I had to prune my brain into a very specific place in order to understand how to run my setup. People look at my equipment and ask me, "how do you remember what everything does?" And I think that's a great question. I look at a guitar player and think, "how do you remember where all those notes are on the fretboard?" And how do you remember how to move your fingers in all these different ways? That's equally complex.

I think the connections there are all long shots, maybe dealing with more intuitive things.

Can you reveal some of your less obvious influences? What artistic things influence your creative practice, other than synthesizer music?

Peter Brook is a huge influence on me. I named a record after his book *The Empty Space*. It really flipped my wig, a lot. Talking about specifically the role of the performer, the role of the audience, and the different ways we can present performance to people and what they mean.

One that people may not guess just from hearing my music, but would know if they know my career in general, would be reggae—it's huge. Especially dub music and guys

"I want to be able to play a full show, no compromises, with stuff I can carry onto an airplane, because I would never check any of my stuff."

like Scratch and Scientist. The idea of "studio as instru-
ment" and extended technique recording is huge.

For other stuff, it gets tricky. I try to think about what
I'm putting in the tank, and what's coming out. If anything
it's things like the Grateful Dead. A huge inspiration to me,
but not in any way you could hear. In the way it inspires me
to want to make music, it inspires me to want to hear music.

FOUR

How do you maintain engagement with your synthesizer?

A big part of that is spending time away from my in-
strument, and spending time away from it. I definitely get
frustrated with it, I think everybody does, with any instru-
ment. After a while you feel like you're beating your head
against a wall.

I do really enjoy being able to inject some new fun into
your instrument for a low price, but in the past year or so
I've slowed considerably on the sort of acquisition front.
Both because I can't afford to keep buying new things, but
also because I really like what I have. There's nothing in my
system I would feel comfortable getting rid of, I don't know
what I'd take out of the case to make room for something
new. I don't want to have a performance system that's any
bigger than my travel case.

I want to be able to play a full show, no compromises,
with stuff I can carry onto an airplane, because I would
never check any of my stuff. That's a nightmare. That's
why I bought the case I have—it's the most Eurorack you
can fit in an overhead compartment.

*You seem very open in general about sharing what equip-
ment you use to make your music, in a synth world that often*

seems protective when it comes to how the music is made. I think to a degree that there's a fear that if you know what gear was used, you'll be able to recreate the sound, but also I think there's a value in keeping things mysterious and unknowable that's being protected.

I get that people are wary about talking about their gear too much. The thing about the modular synth renaissance going on right now that I'm most excited about is that as this equipment gets more and more common, those of us who use it as tools to make music won't be defined by our instruments. Maybe this is me being a prick, but I don't want people to think of me as being a modular synth musician—I want people to think of me as being a musician.

I see in the synth world a contingent of people who have never played a show, never made a record, and generally treat their synthesizer like it's a toy. And I want to be totally clear—I don't think there's anything wrong with that, at all. If you build the best modular system and you keep it in your house and play with it like a toy, good on you. But I understand that the manufacturers are, to a degree, maybe a little more interested in hearing from the working musicians. Which is funny, because it's the other dudes who are the most vocal, and it's the other dudes who are keeping everyone in business.

Is there any dream gear you have? If you had an unlimited budget.

More than anything, I'd spend money on really nice recording gear. Instrument wise, Waldorf XT. Prophet VS. At this point, all the stuff I really want is so different from the stuff I have. I'd never get mad at finding a Jupiter 8 or a Yamaha CS-80 or something like that, but it's not the thing I salivate over. I'm not dreaming about that. I want the wackiest digital synths. I've been borrowing a rack-mount Waldorf XT for a while and I love it. I really want a keyboard polyphonic synth. I have a Super JX that I love but it's fucked up, the memory got corrupted. That is a really good pad synth, though it doesn't have the craziness of the

"I'm really obsessed with the idea of doing polyphony in a modular setting, which is a fool's errand."

A POLOPHONIC SYNTH is any synthesizer capable of playing multiple, independent notes simultaneously.

"When I'm working with a human played instrument, I want it to sound less human. And vice versa."

Waldorf stuff.

Nobody is making a Eurorack eight-stage loopable envelope for wavetable position. It's such a different experience, after programming synths in such a particular way, to be able to touch a button and call up a pre-set I made. And the modulation stuff you can do with those things is so deep. In terms of modular stuff—I really want a Buchla 200E system one day. I don't know if I'll ever get one, because it's the type of thing I'd never take out of the house. But once I got one, I'd probably never leave the house so—problem solved.

What are your current interests within the realm of synthesis? Everyone's system is so idiosyncratic in some ways, and it seems like everyone has a pet project, a patch they've envisioned and are trying to pull together.

The past year I've spent a lot of time working on this four-voice thing, and that's been kind of my obsession. It started with the Synthesizer Technologies E102 Digital Shift Register, which is a shift register that allows you to have delay in-between the steps, so you can introduce voltage to change the timing. It's a really flexible way to turn a sequence into four voices.

So I got that, and I built a four voice system around that. Four Make Noise STO's, an Intellijel Quadra, a Make Noise QMMG, and then everything's being sequenced from the Antimatter Audio Brain Seed. I basically plugged a keyboard in and played as if it was a keyboard monosynth, recorded that into the Brain Seed, a three or four hundred note sequence of me playing. I clock everything to one clock source, and use the probability mode on Noise Engineering Zularic Repetitor to trigger the four different envelopes on the Quadra.

What I really wanted was a way to take a simple sequence, transpose it across four voices, and then have it constantly be shifting and changing. Rather than introducing random voltage into the quantizer and summing it like I'd normally do, instead I'm using the same patterns of notes and smearing the way they move across the four voices via the E102. Coupled with random patterns of gates from the Repetitor, you always end up with something that sounds remarkably musical.

I got really obsessed with that combination, maybe partially because I'm really obsessed with the idea of doing polyphony in a modular setting, which is a fool's errand. This is a weird workaround for that, and I just love the way it sounds. I love modulating the clock in a smooth, natural way and the whole thing starts to feel really played, really human. It feels like someone performing on a keyboard in a really natural way I've never been able to get out of the synth before. It feels way more human.

Would you say you're interested in blurring the boundary between natural or human performance and machine generated performance?

Ideally when you listen to a record you wouldn't know, or it doesn't matter. I think that's more the point, actually. It doesn't matter how I made it. It shouldn't matter how I made it. What matters is what it is. When I'm working with a human played instrument, I want it to sound less human. And vice versa. I'm always trying to push things out of the spaces you expect them to be in, because that's where you find interesting stuff. That's where you hit the ideas that are more uniquely yours, things other people aren't exploring as much.

It's like a little arms race with this stuff, because there's a lot of people getting into it right now and those of us who've been into it for a while and have a couple years on the general modular public are working extra hard to stay ahead of the curve. I'm looking at all these kids buying all this crazy, expensive shit—spending money in a way I definitely can't afford to do because I'm a working musician—and I don't want some kid to be able to buy a better sounding synth than I can make on my own.

I don't know. I don't really worry about that, but every once in awhile, in the deepest corners of my mind, it starts to come up a little bit.

A GATE is a binary control signal that has an on and off state, used to transmit rhythmic information within a synthesizer system.

"Maybe this is me being a prick, but I don't want people to think of me as being a modular synth musician—I want people to think of me as being a musician."

> *There's definitely this phenomenon, when you think of a really good idea on an instrument that doesn't require physical virtuosity in the traditional sense like a synthesizer, there's this intellectual property question. It's not like you're Steve Howe from Yes and you write "Clap" and can say, "just try and play it, dumb-ass" with a smirk. And yet, there's an element of taste that can't be purchased and it transcends all equipment.*

I've had friends of mine who like the stuff I make, and asked me, "what are you using?" And I'm perfectly happy to tell them, and I walk them through the whole setup, and a couple of them go and buy that stuff. And they call me a month later to tell me it still doesn't sound like my stuff and all I can say is, "no shit." It doesn't sound like me because I'm not there.

Being able to build a very individualized instrument closes the gap a little bit. If you want to know how I'm making particular sounds, I can tell you the pieces. I can tell you how they're put together. But the decision of what sounds to make is unteachable; You can't teach taste. You can't teach creativity.

> *I'm pretty sure they're working on that at the Waldorf School.*

I always struggle with how to talk about this without sounding like an asshole saying, "I'm better than everybody," because that's definitely not the way I feel.

> *But that is what makes good musicians, right? They're better at music than bad musicians?*

I do think to have any sort of success, whether on a professional level or on a personal, interior level with your art, you need a little bit of ego. Without it you're never going to understand that what you're doing is important. You're never going to have the misguided thought that what you're doing is important, which is so necessary. Especially when you're starting out, and what you're doing probably isn't

"It drives me crazy when I listened to stuff I recorded even six months ago, and I think, 'what the fuck was I doing?'"

that important. But you gotta get over that hump.

I don't know—it's a weird thing. You can't buy it. It's not for sale, really. But some of the more basic techniques that I use, I could explain to someone and they could pick up and deploy them, and get an approximation of my thing. Certainly close enough. People call me and say, "I heard this guy's record, you should file a lawsuit." And I say, "Really though? Because I can name at least twenty people that I was ripping that idea off from."

That sort of creativity aspect of synthesizer music, of having to make something very new, is pretty unique to electronic music. Nobody is going up to rock bands and telling them, "you have to rewrite the way we think about this! Use these instruments to make sounds nobody had heard before!" Nobody wants that. It's been done. We already had U.S. Maple, nobody needs to do that again.

Now with really immediate ways of disseminating musical ideas, like making an Instagram video of a patch, people can figure out what's going on in a patch and recreate it pretty quickly. They just have to pause the video enough times.

If they can do that, they shouldn't be wasting their time copying my sounds, they should focus on their own work. Because I can't even do that, I can't even recreate things I've documented like that. It drives me crazy when I listened to stuff I recorded even six months ago, and I think, "what the fuck was I doing?"

I listen to stuff I made when I had much less equipment— three oscillators, one sequencer, a Make Noise QMMG, one Maths, and I listen to that record constantly thinking, "How did I do that? I have no idea how I did that. That I'm pretty sure I know how I did but I can't do it again." I wanted to do some of those pieces live, so I'd spend hours listening to those recordings and gathering all the information from them I could, and I never even came close to getting anything like the original. Whenever I even came close I'd end up with some ugly baby that nobody wanted, this awful thing.

"...an instrument that's as unwieldy as these things are [has] as much willpower or influence over you...as you have over it."

> "I use the melody aspect of my work a lot of times as a camouflage tarp to cover the other aspects of it."

Did that process, or failed process, teach you something about your synthesizer practice?

That's when I realized the best way for me to work was to always start from the ground up. That became my process. Sitting down with three ideas, just to get started, and from there just playing and seeing what I find, what's interesting to me right now. It's a hard thing to translate into live performance because a lot of the things I find interesting in my home studio environment are not interesting in the same way when I'm in front of people. Sometimes I find I have a hard time focusing or having the patience to do things I would do if I was at home, things I know sound good and would work well if I have the patience to let them happen. But you get all amped up, man.

Your 45-minute set at home that you rehearsed turns into eighteen minutes live.

Yeah! And most of the time people are stoked if you play a short set at a show, especially at a D.I.Y. show. "Oh, you didn't play for forty five minutes? Thank fucking god, maybe we'll be out of here before 2:00 a.m." But I've been in the position too where I'm doing a bigger show, or the opening slot for somebody, and I'm supposed to play for forty five minutes and I play for twenty eight minutes and that's it. I'm out, I'm done, I've got nothing. And I just fucked the whole show up for everybody. I mean, not really, but kind of!

What are your thoughts on the role of chance in synthesizer composition?

It's a huge thing for me. Maybe the primary source of my interest in it. There is definitely a tendency for people working with modular synthesizers, with sequencers to produce music that prominently features repeating patterns and cycles. I think that can be really boring. Sometimes that's exactly where you want to be, but I think the whole point of working with an instrument that's as unwieldy as these things are is that they have as much willpower or influence over you as the performer as you have over it. Chance is a huge part of that process, and a huge part of what makes synthesizers so interesting to me.

Writing in elements of chance, of randomness, and allowing for processes that are not synchronized that create different juxtapositions as they move. Even simple things like three different frequency LFO's, they're going to keep moving and combining in new ways. Modular synthesis really points people down that path because one of the strong suits of the instrument is there was so much effort put into designing randomizing elements in it.

A LOW-FREQUENCY OSCILLATION (LFO) refers to a slowly cycling oscillator, the output of which is used to control another parameter.

For a long time my main composition tool was combining random voltages with a sequencer in different ratios to create patterns that didn't just loop and repeat endlessly. Notes in a scale that you define, but the pattern is beyond your control in a certain way. You hear elements coming back around, and you start to perceive patterns, but those patterns are in flux. In the end, the patterns are just a delivery method for the sound, for the environment, for that experience.

I use the melody aspect of my work a lot of times as a camouflage tarp to cover the other aspects of it. Once you wrap it in melody, it looks like a more traditional piece of music than it really is. It gets you in the door. I want to be surprised by my instrument. I want to be entertained by my instrument. Part of the reason why I make music is to entertain myself, at a very basic level. I'm entertained by the instrument when it pushes back and does things I don't expect it to do.

Do you think about what to do with your body when you play live?

I think a lot about what people are looking at. I've experimented a lot with playing on the floor instead of on the stage, since there's nothing in my rig that's gonna feed back. Why not just put me in front of the PA, so I can hear it exactly as the audience hears it? And often when I do that

> "I look up from the synthesizer at the audience and think, 'these people don't actually realize that I'm playing music right now.'"

I'll also play with my back to the audience, so my instrument is facing them too, and they're looking at my rig the way I see it. I think that's honestly probably more interesting for most people than looking at the top half of my face over my case, and I'm mostly hidden. My dream would be to play at the soundboard in the back of the house though.

I've done performances with visual elements before, projections and stuff. I think the lack of visual material is in some ways a weakness. I've done so many tours and shows with rock bands, and while there's definitely a certain segment of the population, certain clubs even, where nobody is going to think it's weird that you're up there with a box full of wires, twirling knobs, it's not the majority. I look up from the synthesizer at the audience and think, "these people don't actually realize that I'm playing music right now." They don't understand what's going on. People have come up to me while I'm playing a set and made requests, like I was the DJ. I was playing a show in LA a few years ago, and I had just set up and started playing and a girl came up to me and started talking to me while I was performing. She asked me to play "Rock Lobster."

FIVE

Do you think there is any real distinction in performance at an essential level between a synthesizer and any other instrument?

Bringing it all back around to the beginning, I think there is this assumption that electronic musicians don't work as hard as other kinds of musicians. But I'd say 99% of all musicians don't work as hard as the 1% who work really hard, so I think it's across the board. It's easier to get away with for electronic artists though maybe, because you have more a technological assist. Less so with the synths maybe, more with the computer. Things like Ableton are designed to prevent you from making bad, or at least unpalatable, music.

I go back and forth on this. When you see the older generation of experimental dudes, almost all of them are just doing playback. None of them are performing live. And when you look at the tradition of western avant-garde music, so much of it was made in such a way that the only method to present it is playback. And I think there's definitely a huge stigma against that, but I think that if the audience doesn't know, I don't think it matters.

I played a show a year or two ago with Curtis Roads, and he straight up just played a stereo track out of audacity on his laptop. And it was fucking great! And you know what? This dude probably spent more time working on that piece of music than any of these other motherfuckers have spent working on music in their entire lives! I'm not gonna tell him he can't do that.

I think your main job as the presenter of music is to present a strong, powerful experience, and you can use any tools at your disposal to do that. I don't have a problem using pre-recorded elements in my sets, especially if it's something that allows me to make a much higher quality presentation of music. I don't feel comfortable just hitting play and sitting there and listening, I need to have some level of interaction, but what's great about my setup is that I can do that. I can have a track playing and have it interact with the synth in different ways.

Your only responsibility as a performer is not to prove to everybody how good you are at your instrument. Your job, or at least my job, is to create a powerful experience. To give people a really strong reaction to what you're doing.

Gifted & Blessed

Gabriel Reyes-Whittaker, also known as Gifted & Blessed, is an intellectually engaged student of synthesizer music and a talented, evocative composer in his own right. This list is his essential curriculum of the music that has intrigued him and impacted his own work as of the publishing of this book.

guide

to

the

essentials

~~~~~~

Terry Riley, *Shri Camel*

This recording opened me to the possibilities of alternate tunings for synthesizer and was one of my first experiences with drone elements in electronic music at a young age. This recording is a good example of demonstrating the synthesizer not just as a cool sounding novelty but also as a means for communicating the deeper spiritual possibilities of music using pure electronic tones. One can hear the depth of Terry Riley's life practice.

Steve Roach, *Dreamtime Return*

Much of Steve Roach's catalog displays a masterful and singular approach to creating sonic environments through synthesis, but this recording in particular made me aware that he had been exploring primal and ancestral earth sounds in combination with the sounds of modern analog synthesis long before I ever came along. I have been privileged to get to know Steve a bit and to experience and share in his recording process. *Dreamtime Return* is one of the timeless recordings that seems to be relevant at all times.

Stevie Wonder, *Music of My Mind*

This is Stevie's first record with T.O.N.T.O. (The Original New Timbral Orchestra synthesizer) and its creators, Malcolm Cecil and Bob Margouleff. This record exemplifies the best of analog synthesis in pop music, surely one of the best and most original programming of modular synths along with powerfully inventive songwriting. "Superwoman," for example, is a masterpiece. There's nothing cheesy or phony about this album. All of Stevie's TONTO recordings are super tasteful and inspired many synth nerds like myself over time.

Tom Dissevelt & Kid Baltan, *The Fascinating World of Electronic Music*

These guys are heroes of mine who inspired so much of the electronic music that followed them. Things they were doing in the 1950s still sound modern and totally unique, as is the case with this album. Also the compositions are tasteful and fun so again, not just simply a bunch of cool quirky electronic sounds. All the sounds were one of a kind as well since they designed and built everything themselves.

Jon Appleton, *Four Fantasies for Synclavier*

Jon Appleton was one of the pioneers behind the New England Digital Synclavier synthesizer in the late '70s and early '80s. This album (and his others on this same synthesizer) show some of the amazing possibilities of the Synclavier which haven't necessarily all been improved on or surpassed completely in the modern digital age. This is the area and era of digital synthesis that sounds really beautiful to me.

60

Hugh Hopper   Alan Gowen   Europa Records

Two Rainbows Daily

Philip Glass, *North Star*

This of course is not a purely synthesized album. It does include organ and other instrumentation, but Philip does play an Arp synth on this record that is absolutely beautiful. This is one of the records that made me want to buy a synthesizer.

ARP Instruments, Inc. was an American manufacturer of synthesizers founded iby Alan Robert Pearlman in 1969.

Hugh Hopper & Alan Gowen, *Two Rainbows Daily*

This is a record that I first came across through my interest in the bands National Health and Soft Machine (which Alan Gowen and Hugh Hopper played in, respectively), but I encountered it again when the late great Jay Dee sampled it for Common's "Nag Champa." Revisiting the record, I realized how beautifully the synthesizer was used on this album by Alan Gowen. Most solo or duo synthesizer records focus on either drones or wonky sounds, not the lush jazz and prog-minded compositional structures that Alan Gowen and Hugh Hopper were exploring. Still a favorite.

Here, DRONE refers to a note or chord that is continuously sounded throughout most or all of a piece.

Eliane Radigue, *Songs of Milarepa*

This is another recording which inspires me in Eliane Radigue's use of pure electronic tones. So subtle. It is another excellent exemplification of the synthesizer as a vehicle for meditation or spiritual practice. This feels like the essence of the position of Milarepa in his awareness.

The Other People Place, *Lifestyles of the Laptop Café*

Around the time I had first gotten comfortable with MIDI sequencing and had gotten a few starter drum machines and synths, a friend introduced me to the music of the late great James Stinson and Drexciya, starting with this album. This record is the perfect introduction to the very complex and varied body of work put forth by Drexciya under various monikers. It is a very minimal, seemingly simple approach to soulful techno music. It is another record that never seems to age. Although I didn't try to repeat what was done with this project, it did inspire a lot of my approach to sequencing at that time.

Sun Ra, *The Magic City*

A CLAVIOLINE is an early electrical keyboard, a precursor of modern analog synthesizers.

This record features Sun Ra on a very primitive version of a synthesizer called the clavioline, which had never been played in the context of jazz. It open my ears to so-called "space jazz" and an approach to electronic music outside of time using more of the uncommon shades in the spectrum of all the possible musical colors, which was helped greatly by the inclusion of the clavioline.

6 1/2 questions for

c & g

Critter & Guitari, the team of Owen Osborn and Chris Kucinski, make beautiful, functionally-rich musical instruments that bridge the worlds of audio, video, analog, and digital synthesis, in such a way that they seem to exist uncannily in a colorful, euphoric world all their own.

1. What is the spirit or philosophy of C&G? Is it to be distinct, or create instruments according to certain guiding principles, or just to create the best instruments you can? What do you look for in a new design?

Chris: A C&G instrument must be fun! And a big part of music making for us is the exploration. We started out exploring music together and gradually making instruments became the thing we explore. I hope that our instruments spark exploration and experimentation. However you use one is cool by us.

Owen: The instruments mostly arise out of a process of experimentation and exploration. There isn't much thought about trying to make something new or unique initially, just trying to have fun working with material that interests us. In fact we do a fair amount of reinventing wheels. Eventually we'll happen upon something that other people are excited about too.

2. What was your introduction to synthesis/synthesizers? Do you have strong memories/associations with certain pieces of hardware, even if you don't own them anymore?

Chris: It wasn't audio synthesis, but doing Logo at computer lab in elementary school was as formative as those things go. I couldn't wait to go back there and program (without knowing what that really meant!) the "turtle" do some cool stuff on the screen. That's essentially what we're up to today!

Owen: I remember plugging an old drum machine into a TV set when I was little, and finding the patterns mesmerizing. That you could see the sound and it was all part of the same phenomenon was so cool, and I just wanted to do more of that. Sadly I sold the drum machine at a yard sale for 20 bucks which was so stupid.

LOGO was an educational programming language designed in 1967 by Daniel G. Bobrow, Wally Feurzeig, Seymour Papert and Cynthia Solomon.

3. How do you conceive of electronic instruments vis-à-vis their relationship to older musical technologies?

Chris: It's better to think of 'now' instead of the past. We can only work in the present.. I'm excited by the future and enjoy history, but those time frames can only help so much today! That said, it is important to pay attention to previous iterations of musical and/or technological ideas. Older electronic instruments typically have more inherent constraints (technological or otherwise) and it's good to remember that when we're working on something new – simple is good too!

[Owen]

3 1/2. What about their relationship to nature or the natural world? Do you draw any inspiration from your observations of nature or the natural world?

Chris: Of course! Our newest instrument is called the 'Organelle.' The name suggests "little organ" and it also refers to the specialized parts inside cells. You can customize the Organelle by adding different patches (modes) to it. I know that's not how cells work, but I like the idea that these modes comprise the bigger idea of the instrument – tiny parts that create a whole. When I first learned of organelles in high school, I remember my classmates and I had our favorite ones. The instrument was going to be like that: a cell with many functions, but some functions would be more interesting to different people: vacuole vs ribosome :: sampling vs synthesizing, etc.

Owen: Not specific observations, but there are elements in nature that influence our process. Feedback and iteration are big ones. For example using a few Kaleidoloop (sound recorders) to bounce sound around, recording while others are playing, then switching it up. The sounds become infused with their environment and take on a lifelike quality, similar to how natural systems evolve.

4. What kind of instrument, or feature of an instrument, do you dream of creating using technology which has not yet been developed?

Chris: I was joking with someone who recently came by our studio that we'll be done making instruments when we make one that reads minds.

Owen: Working with electronics and computers can be such a pain sometimes, and I am always wondering if there isn't a quicker way to speed up the process, so we could create these electronic/computer music systems in a more fluid way. Then making the music and making the instrument would really become one. We like to say it is all the same, that some artists use their instruments or write out music freehand, and our medium is electronic circuits and computer code. But the problem is using computers and electronics can introduce many distractions and frustrations. Nick Bostrom writes about a kind of superintelligence that has a module for writing software. It just spews out computer code as easily as we chew food. So that would be the technology I would want: some kind of mind upgrade that would allow me to write code and design electronics without having to think about it.

6. Can you describe with as much detail as possible your own personal synth practice? What do you work with, where and when do you work? How does playing synthesizers fit into your lives?

Chris: The more instruments we make, the less we play. It is unfortunate. But when I get a quiet moment in the studio, it's great to get weird with whatever's on the work table.

Owen: Mostly making the instruments and playing the instruments become part of the same music making process. Although these days it is a lot of making instruments and

Chris [cont.] Because it is not something that happens everyday, I think I end up making better/weirder sounds than if I did it constantly – fewer self-imposed rules!

Owen [cont.] not creating as much sound (see #5). But we are excited about the new Organelle which allows one to create new patches and sounds much more easily.

6. What would you say to someone who is curious about synthesizers but has not started to experiment with them?

Chris: Go for it! Synths are so much fun. And if you can get into the math behind them, it's even better – it's another way to understand the world.

Owen: Just dive in and start playing around. It is better to start with simple stuff first to get a handle on how everything works. You don't need tons of knobs or modules or programs to get cool stuff happening.

Olivier Gillet's work extends beyond the creation of synthesizers into realms of pure imaginative possibility. After my first reading of this material, I began to develop the distinct impression that the terrifically unique musical equipment he creates is in some way only a byproduct of some deeper, more essential investigations.

SCIENCE

It is difficult for me to conceive of an intersection between science and music because they exist on entirely different planes. I am not saying that we have here two fields that are completely apart – but that science is not a "field" in itself, but rather, a kind of discourse. Science is a way of looking at things, a process for getting at knowledge, a recipe for being inquisitive; and as such, one can be scientific with everything – I can be scientific with signals from far-away galaxies or what is in my dinner plate or with the grammar of rhetorical questions in Jewish-American novels.

One can be scientific with music too – let us take measurements to determine which ratios of string lengths create pleasing tones and see if there is a mathematical pattern, and Pythagoras was already doing this without synthesizers! There is a long tradition of scientists and composers being inquisitive and methodical with music, and I don't see it as the specificity of electronic music. Indeed, it would be wrong to categorize electronic music as "scientific" – it would exclude other modes of inquiry like spirituality, sensuality or psychedelics which all played and continue to play a role in electronic music's evolution.

If it is not in this (non-existent) intersection, where is the locus of electronic music? The intersection of music and technology might be a better definition, but I see two limitations there. First, that the practice of electronic music might or might not involve a relationship with technology – I am free to ignore the technological dimension of the instrument and take it as a natural artifact with which I will develop an intuitive, sensual relationship. The second is that the cello and the saxophone were, in their time, crazy, futuristic technological innovations, and thus, advanced technology is not the prerogative of electronic music.

What if we said that electronic music is the music made with our era's most advanced technology? But then I won-

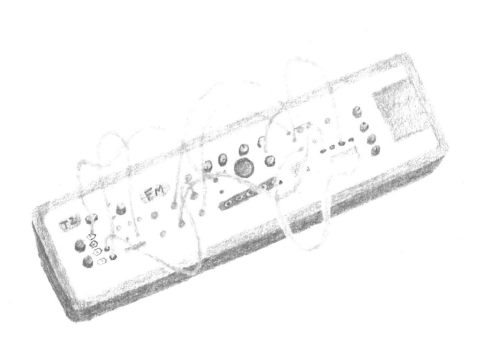

der what will happen in a few decades when the most efficient computational devices no longer use electrons as a medium. Will we talk about "photonic music," "quantum music" or "computational music"? Will "electronic music" become dated and synonymous with "music created with the kind of laughably archaic electron-based information processing equipment which was state of the art between 1950 and 2050"?

It is quite interesting to see to which extent some instrument designers celebrate or fetishize the scientific aspect—naming their modules the "Non-Euclidean phase synchronizer-Model 420D" or adopting some of the design idiosyncrasies of lab equipment (graduations, vernier potentiometers, austere look). It is most of the time tongue-in-cheek geekiness, but I wonder sometimes if this interferes with the kind of relationship we have with the instruments, if this unnecessarily pushes us towards an experimental approach, or make us yearn for certain places and times.

"As if pianos grew on trees!"

A VERNIER POTENTI-
OMETER is a device for
measuring voltage and
current.

NATURE

Such a treacherous word.

Synthesizers do not live in the realm of ideas, or in worlds of fiction: they are first class citizens of the natural world, they are tangible, made of copper and baked sand! It is infuriating to hear people draw a line between "natural" pianos and "synthetic" synthesizers (and it is not just laypersons who are doing that—check the vocabulary used by Moog and Steinway when they describe their products). As if pianos grew on trees! There should be a fourth law from Clarke that would state: "Any sufficiently ancient technology is indistinguishable from nature."

Agriculture used to be cutting-edge technology, and there

Science Fiction author
ARTHUR C. CLARKE'S
so-called third law of
prediction is generally
formulated as, "Any suf-
ficiently advanced tech-
nology is indistinguish-
able from magic."

A SAWTOOTH WAVE is
a kind of non-sinusoidal
waveform named for its
distinctly saw-like look.

"We had to wait for the 20th century for the chiasmus to operate — visual arts finally became abstract and music concrete."

A SIGNAL PATH is
the route an audio or
control signal follows
through a circuit or se-
ries of circuits.

is so little of our world that hasn't been shaped by our technological civilization. All this to say that what we call "nature" is as synthetic, technological, and stained by *Homo sapiens sapiens* as a sawtooth wave is. The relationship between synthesizers and earlier instruments always reminds me of the arbitrariness of the notion of nature, but also, as stated above, that the synthetic "sci-fi-ness" of synthesizers is just a construct.

Let us try to push this topic of "nature" into another direction, let us narrow down our view of "nature" to the phenomena we can assume predated our species — trees, rain, rocks...What immediately strikes me is the opposite trajectory of music and visual arts. For centuries visual arts perfected the accurate — photorealistic I would say — representation of nature, while music remained extremely abstract and only at rare occasions mimicked naturally occurring sounds — as if nature looked beautiful but sounded ugly. We had to wait for the 20th century for the chiasmus to operate — visual arts finally became abstract and music concrete.

What can we learn from the sounds emerging from natural processes? The two most significant dimensions to me are those of texture, and randomness. For centuries, musical investigations were very compartmented: below 5 Hz and it is rhythm, the domain of the composer. Below 50 Hz and it is melody/harmony, the domain of the composer again; or timbre, the domain of the luthier — and there is a kind of no man's land in-between which nobody explored. Music resembled cathedrals — a grand architecture, ridiculously detailed stained glass, but emptiness in-between. Note that many traditional synthesizers have their signal paths and parameter ranges similarly compartmented.

To me, that's the most striking feature of music as it existed until the 20th century — the first thing that visitors from outer space would detect if they poked at it with their Fourier appendages. And the strangest thing is that this is in this range that the "natural" sounds are the richest, that we feel and experience the manyness and rawness of nature.

Why have we been so scared of it? Because of the ambiguity? (This vibration, is it rhythm, is it pitch?) The other striking thing is the importance of randomness. Check a definition of "music" and there is a good chance you will see something about "ordering" or""organization." What we can learn from natural sounds is that there can be beauty, or expressivity in their apparent lack of organization.

We can create beauty not by arranging sounds, but by arranging random processes generating sounds. The connections between these two lessons from nature–(microsonic) texture and randomness–are so deep. One can't really think about one without getting to the other. Xenakis or Mandelbrot were always moving back and forth between these two notions–the stochastic and the "rich at all scales."

This is an area in which I think there are still tools to be invented–what kind of signal processing operations can we invent to make interesting things happen at the scale of texture?

PRACTICE

I rarely practice playing the synthesizer, I mostly practice "making" synthesizers. One can often read about various synthesizer designers building the instruments they need for their own musical ideas, but this is something I avoid doing. I am scared of "overfitting"–of making something that nobody else could ever make on their own–and machine learning taught me that keeping things simple is a good insurance policy. I am rarely on good terms with a module once I finish it, and knowing intimately absolutely every single line of code or bit of schematics inside a module breaks the spell. In other words, it feels way too uncanny to play my own modules once they are finished and in production.

"Xenakis or Mandelbrot were always moving back and forth between these two notions— the stochastic and the 'rich at all scales.'"

PURE DATA (PD) and SUPERCOLLIDER are popular computer programs for simulating, among other diverse things, audio synthesis.

An OSCILLOSCOPE is an electronic device for rendering audio waveforms visible on a screen.

"I guess it is even more hypnotic to look at all those red and blue traces when it is dark outside."

In terms of workflow, designing synthesizers includes extremely varied tasks: gathering ideas, exploring concepts on paper or with prototyping tools like pd or supercollider, researching digital signal processing methods, writing code, designing circuit boards and bringing them up, and the tedious phase during which I tune/balance things until they sound or feel right to me. All this within the constraint of running a profitable business.

All these tasks have their own routines and I am extremely sensitive to the working conditions. Solving some of the technical problems involved during the development of a circuit or module requires me to be "in the flow" – some tasks need intense, uninterrupted concentration for four or five hours. I used to be the hardcore guy who thinks that if you don't have an oscilloscope at home, you're not an engineer, but it really improved my quality of life when I decided to do all the development in a space that was not my home, at normal day hours. These days, there is only one exception left – circuit board design, which I do at night, at home, in one long 5 or 6 hour marathon – I guess it is even more hypnotic to look at all those red and blue traces when it is dark outside.

The most interesting thing in terms of workflow is maybe that 95% of the module development process happens in my head. I have a pool of a dozen new ideas that I envision in my mind – I picture how the modules would look, what they do, how they do it, how I would explain or describe what they do – but they all have a problem or something I am not satisfied with – they are not original enough, or there is a technical challenge I have to overcome, or I have doubts about which parameters to expose or how many inputs/outputs they should have.

Almost every hour of the day, as a kind of background task, while I do the dishes or go out running or pack boxes of modules for my dealers, I pick a module from this virtual rack, look at it and think about its "problem." Whenever a solution is found, there is this phase of sudden excitement in which all the hardware and 95% of the code is written in a matter of weeks, if not days, and after that, 5 or 6 months of dread, doubts, and balancing. It goes slow, ridiculously fast, then slow – but I guess all creative processes are like that.

FUTURE / INTERESTS

I have taken the freedom of grouping together the topics of the future and my interests because for me, they coincide. I am in a position where I can make some of my predictions about the future of synthesis happen. It is not as much "where are we headed?" as "where should we be heading and what should I do to get there?" My predictions are just my current areas of research.

One idea I am exploring at the moment stems from a very simple question: what are we trying to do when we adjust the knobs of a synthesizer? One point of view would be to say that this is a musical gesture – just like I would move my finger on a string to create a vibrato. The synthesis parameters are a set of possibilities of "gestures" for expressively altering sound. From this point of view, it is difficult to innovate or change things – if you ever decide to make this or that parameter disappear, it would seem like you would deprive the musician of an opportunity for self-expression. At the other extreme, the knobs could be seen as instrument design tools – the chisel of the luthier, no need to touch anything once they are all set. The preset culture of the 90s put the emphasis on that. I am trying to look at parameters from a third angle, that of a man-machine dialogue: I want this result, a result I can already hear in my mind, let me adjust the knobs to get there. Would there be other ways of describing what we want to hear? I wish synthesizers could sense or listen to examples of what we

"Instead of a red 'rec' button recording one instance (of a sound, a melody, a gesture...), music equipment should have a purple 'learn' button..."

VIBRATO is the rapid, slight variation in the pitch of an audio signal.

want them to do. One way would be through intelligent use of sensors – imagine tapping, scratching or caressing something to convey various kinds of envelopes, performing the gestures for the first few notes and then the synthesizer "gets it" and takes over for the next notes, because it can understand the gist of the gesture and the part of variability and randomness in it. Audio analysis would be another way to get there – from recorded sounds, we should be able to sample parameters, sound trajectories, not just the audio signal itself. But the word "sampling" is too limiting and conveys the wrong concept, as it carries the idea of recording and replaying literally. Instead of a red "rec" button recording one instance (of a sound, a melody, a gesture...), music equipment should have a purple "learn" button recording several occurrences that would simultaneously capture the essence and the opportunities for random divergence of what we have played. The recent advances in machine learning could make this a reality very soon.

Back to the very act of twiddling a knob. Could it also sometimes mean "take me somewhere else?" So far, navigating the space of sounds offered by a synthesizer could only be done in two ways: traveling along the narrow path of a parameter – continuous, more or less congruent with a perceptual parameter – or the disaster of loading preset parameters – discrete, without any sense of context of continuity. I am interested in the possibility of a synthesizer interface being a well-organized map of sounds, with continuous travel across all its dimensions. This poses several challenges – should we let the musician learn the map ("with this knob here and this one there, we have this cool place with bellish sounds"), or should we organize things beforehand (a dedicated "make things bellish" knob). And what should the criterion be for deciding what is going to be on the map (analysis of preexisting sounds? or absolutely everything and anything the underlying synthesis technique could produce?). Most importantly, how will the synthesist react to this idea that they are not directly in touch with the underlying sound production process, but are instead steering it in one direction or another? I fear that we are stuck at the level of control and interaction provided by the first analog synthesizers, and that Moog unwillingly established a standard as to what's kosher or not in terms of control or meta-control, about what we feel entitled to be able to control directly or through indirect parameters. So it is perfectly fine to be unable to adjust individual harmonics (spectrum being controlled only by macro operators like "cutoff" and "emphasis"), but as soon as we start talking about meta-parameters or preset morphing for anything else—no, that's unacceptable!

Tangential to the idea of sampling parameters, or the idea of mapping a sound generation process, is the increasing role perception models ("machine listening") will play in synthesis. Historically, perception informed the design of instruments (we give a log scale to a frequency or amplitude knob or CV input because our ear works this way), but I am interested in the possibilities of giving an instrument the ability to hear and analyze its signal path. For example the range and response of a filter could be narrowed down or enlarged depending on whether the signal that enters the filter is harmonically poor or rich. Or constraints could be set—let me tweak the sound in any possible way as long as it won't result in a harsher sound than what it is now. An ideal for me would be a synthesis technique which would not expose anything about the underlying sound generation process (the technical bits—signals, envelopes, operators, waveforms), but which would let me interact directly with the words describing the sound. More science inside for a less "science-y" interface.

All this to say that I would be very surprised if we discovered a radically new class of sound synthesis operations, or a novel way of synthesizing sounds from scratch. More probably, innovation is going to be in the areas of control, interaction—getting the sounds out of our head or our hearts.

At a more personal level, I am currently exploring the connections between algorithmic pattern generation, weaving, and analog video synthesis, through the common themes of the transformation of 1D into 2D, and pattern generation through simple rule systems, but also through similarities they shared in their history. I find it odd that mechanical looms – which were the first examples of programmable pattern generating machines and co-evolved with roller organs, only had a remote influence on the design of our sequencers. What I find fascinating in these old mechanical or even manual processes is that there is a very low upper bound on the complexity of the computational processes at play - it has to be simple, to have a small number of degrees of freedom, for a human or a clunky 19th century machine to do it. That is a quality I value a lot – I like interfaces in which as few knobs as possible engenders something as large and diverse as possible.

ENGAGEMENT

FM, or Frequency Modulation is a process by which one oscillator's timbre is modulated by input from a second oscillator also in the audio range.

FM did not take over subtractive synthesis the same way quantum mechanics took over Bohr's model of the hydrogen atom. We cannot say that such or such synthesis method is the right answer, the ultimate solution. There is no question or problem to be solved in the first place.

Synthesizers are right at the middle of a rubber band, with the elephant of technical innovation constantly pulling one side, and the monkey of culture mischievously wandering on the other. This might explain the odd trajectory, because there is always this possibility of looking back at the past decades and revisiting some of the things we've tried. This is not a bad thing at all, and this might be how the field of synthesis can remain engaging – going forward is not the only allowed move. Subtractive synthesis became fashionable again when we became aware of all the limitations of ridiculously deep ROM-playback synthesis engines; modular systems were probably a reaction to some kind if Ableton Live malaise.

SUBTRACTIVE SYNTHESIS is a method of sound synthesis in which partials of an audio signal are attenuated by a filter to adjust the timbre of a sound.

Like in fashion, there's an equal probability that the next big thing will be a novel idea, or the revival of some 1987 oddity we failed to appreciate back then.

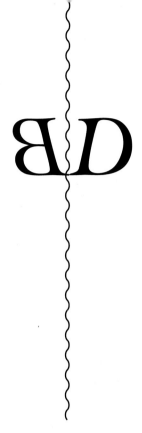

AFTERWORD

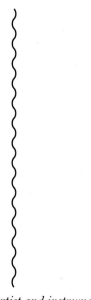

Brian Dewan is an artist and instrument maker.
He lives in Catskill, New York.

Elisha Gray made a musical telegraph.

Thaddeus Cahill dreamed of an instrument that "had the virtues of all instruments and the defects of none."

Leon Theremin made an instrument that you don't touch.

Wendy Carlos said that when people heard the choral parts of Beethoven's Ninth Symphony rendered with a early vocoder, "People looked at us and said, 'Oh, my goodness, what is this?' They were scared by it. They were scared of hearing a chorus of artificial voices."

Don Leslie said, "I'm not an engineer. I was just trying to make the organ sound better."

Pierre Boulez wanted to be surrounded on all sides by controls.

Milton Babbitt said, "Nothing is older than yesterday's futurism."

Hugh LeCaine said, "Many people think of a square wave as being basically unpleasant. But I think of it as having it a poignant, mysterious and rather melancholy quality."

Gyorgy Ligeti said that as a young person in the 1940s he had never heard any electronic music, but he had heard about it, the idea of electronic music was very exciting to him; he had heard that you could create any sound in the electronic music laboratory. When he finally got to the Cologne Studio For Electronic Music, he was disappointed that the equipment was more primitive and limited than he had imagined, and he abandoned electronic music. "But the electronic music studio was a great experience for me, because it changed the way I thought about the orchestra. So now I just write for the orchestra the way I would have used the electronic music studio."

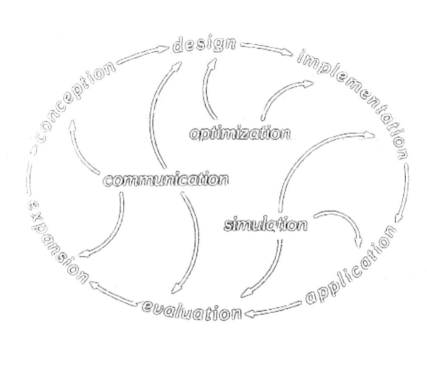

ACKNOWLEDGEMENTS

I'd like to thank everyone who helped to make this book a real thing, and not just something I talk about when people ask me what's new with me and I don't want to admit that nothing really is. That means, first and foremost, Patrick Kiley, intrepid publisher and creator of opportunities to whom I am eternally indebted, who gave me the opportunity to actually do something instead of just talking about it. It also means my family, who are unendingly patient and positive about my work, and my friends, for whose gracious interest and support I owe a debt of gratitude. I'd also like to thank all of the contributors, whose engagement with this project is a large part of what makes it, I hope, good.

"I regard the creation of musical instrumentation as a cyclical, regenerative, evolutionary process, accelerated through optimization and simulation achieved through application of technological resources, and enriched by contact and communication with fellow researchers."

– Don Buchla

[note: This quote, as well as the diagram on page 88, appear on the back of the album *Collaboration in Performance* by Rosenboom & Buchla, 1978.]